Praise for *The Lord's Prayer*

Wesley Hill is by any measure one of the most valuable New Testament interpreters of our time. A respected academic, he is also able to write with the nonspecialist reader in mind, from the perspective of his own God-given, deeply held faith. Most Christians say the Lord's Prayer with great frequency and familiarity, so that we scarcely know what we are saying. In this treasure of a book, Hill opens up the prayer with great freshness for the ordinary reader, so that we seem to hear Jesus himself speaking to us, showing us how to pray to his Father in the same spirit that he himself does. This little volume will enrich a reader's life immeasurably.

Fleming Rutledge
author of *The Crucifixion* and *Help My Unbelief*

When the Lord Jesus teaches his disciples how to pray, he teaches them as a group. They are to pray the Lord's Prayer and they are to pray it together. This book is a sharing in the Lord's own life of prayer that is also a sharing in his disciple Wesley Hill's life of prayer. To pray Christ's prayer with Wesley is to be enriched by the most profound Christian mysteries and to be united to a wide array of pray-ers, stretching out toward God the Father, seeking divine life, love, justice, daily bread, and endurance of trials. Once you have prayed Christ's prayer with Wesley Hill, you will want to do it again and again.

Matthew Levering
Mundelein Seminary
author of *Dying and the Virtues*

This brief guide is a wonderful meditation on the most famous of Christian prayers. At once simple and inexhaustible, the Lord's Prayer is the model of all Christian prayer as well as a mirror of the life of Jesus. For the seeker, beginner, or mature believer, Wesley Hill offers a treasure of wisdom from the saints of the Christian past.

Christopher A. Beeley
Duke Divinity School
author of *Leading God's People*

Wesley Hill's reflection on the Lord's Prayer is elegantly written, theologically astute, and pastorally focused. Hill weaves together insights from Scripture, a variety of theologians past and present, and reflections on the news of the world to paint a revealing picture of what it means to pray this prayer. In so doing, Hill calls us to reflect more deeply—and prayerfully—on the God to whom we pray and the Lord who taught us to pray. This book is worth savoring.

Marianne Meye Thompson
Fuller Theological Seminary,
author of *The God of the Gospel of John*

THE
LORD'S PRAYER

THE LORD'S PRAYER

A Guide to Praying to Our Father

WESLEY HILL

LEXHAM PRESS

The Lord's Prayer: A Guide to Praying to Our Father
Christian Essentials

Copyright 2019 Wesley Hill

Lexham Press, 1313 Commercial St., Bellingham, WA 98225
LexhamPress.com

"Coda: Praying the Lord's Prayer with Rembrandt" is adapted from Wesley Hill, "Praying the 'Our Father' with Rembrandt," *Covenant* blog, September 23, 2015, https://livingchurch.org/covenant/2015/09/23/praying-our-father-rembrandt/. Used by permission.

Unless otherwise noted, Scripture quotations are from the New Revised Standard Version (NRSV), copyright © 1989, National Council of the Churches of Christ in the United States of America. Used by permission. All rights reserved.

Scripture quotations marked (KJV) are from the King James Version. Public domain.

Scripture quotations marked (NEB) are from the New English Bible, copyright © Cambridge University Press and Oxford University Press 1961, 1970. All rights reserved.

Scripture quotations marked (REB) are from the Revised English Bible, copyright © Cambridge University Press and Oxford University Press 1989. All rights reserved.

Rembrandt's *The Return of the Prodigal Son* on page 98 is located at The State Hermitage Museum in St. Petersburg, Russia. Public domain.

Print ISBN 9781683593188
Digital ISBN 9781683593195

Lexham Editorial: Todd Hains, Abigail Stocker, Danielle Thevenaz
Cover Design: Eleazar Ruiz
Typesetting: Abigail Stocker

To Felicity, with all my love

CONTENTS

CHRISTIAN ESSENTIALS

SERIES PREFACE

he Christian Essentials series passes down tradition that matters.

The church has often spoken paradoxically about growth in Christian faith: to grow means to stay at the beginning. The great Reformer Martin Luther exemplified this. "Although I'm indeed an old doctor," he said, "I never move on from the childish doctrine of the Ten Commandments and the Apostles' Creed and the Lord's Prayer. I still daily learn and pray them with my little Hans and my little Lena." He had just as much to learn about the Lord as his children.

The ancient church was founded on basic biblical teachings and practices like the Ten Commandments, baptism, the Apostles' Creed, the Lord's Supper, the Lord's Prayer, and corporate worship. These basics of the Christian life have sustained and nurtured every generation of the faithful—from the apostles to today. They apply equally to old and young, men and women, pastors and church members. "In Christ Jesus you are all sons of God through faith" (Gal 3:26).

We need the wisdom of the communion of saints. They broaden our perspective beyond our current culture and time. "Every age has its own outlook," C. S. Lewis wrote. "It is specially good at seeing certain truths and specially liable to make certain mistakes." By focusing on what's current, we rob ourselves of the insights and questions of those who have gone before us. On the other hand, by reading our forebears in faith, we engage ideas that otherwise might never occur to us.

The books in the Christian Essentials series open up the meaning of the foundations of our faith. These basics are unfolded afresh for today in conversation with the great tradition—grounded in and strengthened by Scripture—for the continuing growth of all the children of God.

Hear, O Israel: The Lord our God, the Lord is one. You shall love the Lord your God with all your heart and with all your soul and with all your might. And these words that I command you today shall be on your heart. You shall teach them diligently to your children, and shall talk of them when you sit in your house, and when you walk by the way, and when you lie down, and when you rise. You shall bind them as a sign on your hand, and they shall be as frontlets between your eyes. You shall write them on the doorposts of your house and on your gates. (Deuteronomy 6:4–9)

OUR FATHER IN HEAVEN,

hallowed be your name,

your kingdom come,

your will be done,

on earth as in heaven.

Give us today our daily bread.

Forgive us our sins

as we forgive those who sin against us.

Save us from the time of trial
and deliver us from evil.

For the kingdom, the power,
and the glory are yours

now and forever.

AMEN.

INTRODUCTION

"Your Father in Secret"

A t the center of Jesus' Sermon on the Mount in the Gospel of Matthew, He offers to His disciples a model for prayer. This would not have seemed at all unusual to Jesus' followers. Many teachers who attracted crowds in Palestine, like Jesus did, were expected to pass on their insights about how best to beseech God, and Jesus wouldn't have raised any eyebrows by conveying His. In the Gospel of Luke, for instance, Jesus' disciples are the ones who prompt His instruction: "Lord, teach us to pray, as John [the Baptist] taught his disciples" (11:1).

What would have been surprising to the crowd listening to Jesus that day was the *way* Jesus spoke about prayer. He rejected the ostentatious style of prayer with which His listeners would have been familiar. Instead, He emphasized how uncomplicated prayer should be:

> And whenever you pray, do not be like the hypocrites; for they love to stand and pray in the synagogues and at the street corners, so that they may be seen by others. Truly I tell you, they have received their reward. But whenever you pray, go into your room and shut the door and pray to your Father who is in secret; and your Father who sees in secret will reward you. When you are praying, do not heap up empty phrases as the Gentiles do; for they think that they will be heard because of their many words. Do not be like them, for your Father knows what you need before you ask him. (Matt 6:5–8)

With these words, Jesus dismisses at a stroke the unusual prayers of the experts in the Jewish law as well as the elaborately theatrical models of the pagan gentile world. There's no need for pretentious displays, Jesus insists. Prayer shouldn't be calculated to impress, whether one is seeking to attract the attention of God or other people. Why? *Because God doesn't need our prayer.* In effect, Jesus says: God isn't looking to have His arm twisted or to be cajoled or bargained with or manipulated. God doesn't require a flawless recitation of certain phrases, as if He were poised to fly into a rage in the absence of the right formula or performance. No, Jesus says, God is "your Father," and He already is disposed favorably toward you. "Before they call I will answer, while they are yet speaking I will hear" (Isa 65:24). Go find a quiet place where you can relax, Jesus seems to say. Unclench your fists. Breathe deeply. Let your heart rate decrease. Know that you're already bathed in the Father's love, and ask simply for what you need, in the assurance that the One to whom you're speaking is already cupping His ear in your direction. *That's* what prayer should be.

It's no wonder, then, that when Christian liturgies introduce the Lord's Prayer in the context of worship, they often use a formula like this: "And now as our savior Christ has taught us, we are bold to say ..." We can, in other words, give up all our anxious efforts to pacify, convince, or haggle with God. We can trade in that performative style of prayer for one that is more homely and familial. As former Archbishop of Canterbury Rowan Williams writes: "We have the nerve to call God what Jesus called him, because of the Spirit we share with Jesus as a result of being baptized, 'immersed' in the life of Jesus."[1] What Jesus—and later Paul, following in His footsteps—offers to believers is a picture of a God who is eager, indeed, delighted to hear prayer. Unlike human fathers, who are often engrossed in their smartphones and have to have their attention captured in some creative way by their children, God is already and always attentive to His children. It is with that in mind that Jesus says to His disciples, "Pray then in this way ..." (Matt 6:9).

T he Lord's Prayer, often called the *Pater Noster* (Latin for "Our Father"), is a kind of template, a "Here, try it this way" sort of prayer. It's a model for approaching God with childlike confidence that He will hear. Depending on who you ask, it is composed of six or seven petitions, the first three focused on God's holy character and rule and the latter three or four concerned with invoking God's help in some way.[2] In what follows, we will inch our way through each petition, drawing on the writings of the church fathers, the Protestant Reformers, and more recent Orthodox, Catholic, and Protestant theologians and preachers to draw out the significance of Jesus' words for Christian prayer today.

Above all, I want to show that the Lord's Prayer is first and foremost about Jesus Himself. Each petition is not only His instruction to His followers about how they are to pray. More fundamentally, each petition is a window into Jesus' own life of prayer—His reliance on and manifestation of the One He called Father. As Dale Allison has put it, "Jesus embodies his speech; he lives as he speaks and speaks as he lives."[3] The Lord's Prayer is a portrait of Jesus Christ—the One who addresses God as Father, who sanctifies God's name, who announces and bears God's healing reign, who submits to God's will, who gives His flesh as daily bread for the life of the world, who provides for the forgiveness of sins through His death on the cross and thus inducts His followers into a lifestyle of forgiveness, and who ultimately delivers believers from the power of death and the devil. Jesus embodies and enacts the prayer He taught His followers to pray.[4] Jesus is "the invisible background of every one of [the Lord's Prayer's] petitions"—all of them are arrows that point toward Him, though He isn't mentioned by name in any of them.[5]

A brief word about translation and inclusive language. I have chosen to use the English Language Liturgical Consultation's 1988 translation of the Lord's Prayer as the primary text that I will comment on here. But I will also reference the familiar King James Version (how could I do otherwise?) as well as newer versions, such as Sarah Ruden's arresting translation.[6] I will also reference, on occasion, my own reading of the Greek versions found in the Gospels of Matthew and Luke.

I have also decided to retain masculine pronouns for God throughout, though I explain at the end of chapter 1 why this must not be understood in a literal way, as if God were male. I also follow the time-honored practice of capitalizing divine pronouns ("He," "His"), in part to signal my belief that while "He" may appropriate our masculine language for His self-communication, God transcends our creaturely categories, and we should not suppose that God's employment of our language is anything other than analogical.[7]

OUR FATHER IN HEAVEN

"OUR FATHER IN HEAVEN"

he God of the Bible creates simply by *speech*. "Let there be light" are God's first spoken words in the book of Genesis (1:3). And unlike the creation myth of ancient Babylon, no feminine consort attends as God utters the world into existence.[8] This creation-by-speaking, as Israel's prophets later underscored, may be pictured with our imagery of fatherhood:

> O LORD, you are our Father;
>> we are the clay, and you are our potter;
>> we are all the work of your hand. (Isa 64:8)

God is the One who gives the world its being, and in that sense God may be said to "Father" it. But at the same time, God's fatherhood is unlike any fatherhood we know on earth. The

Old Testament's use of "Father" for the God of Israel is only a metaphor for God's relationship to His chosen people.[9]

Perhaps the word "only" isn't quite right, though. True, God is not a Father in the way that human fathers are. God, who radically transcends our creaturely categories, is not male (nor is God female, for that matter), and God is not biologically procreative in a human sense. Yet, for all that, the God of Israel chooses the metaphor of fatherhood as one of the prime symbols of His relationship to His people: "I have become a father to Israel, and Ephraim [the northern kingdom] is my firstborn" (Jer 31:9). The Jewish people look back to their deliverance from bondage in Egypt as the moment that sealed their relationship to God as their Father. God had told Moses to say this to Pharaoh, the recalcitrant king of Egypt: "Thus says the LORD: Israel is my firstborn son. I said to you, 'Let my son go that he may worship me'" (Exod 4:22–23). In one of the most beautiful passages of Isaiah, the prophet writes: "You, O LORD, are our father; our Redeemer from of old is your name" (63:16). And, perhaps most poignantly of all, Jeremiah records God's lament over wayward Israel and Judah, borrowing the imagery of a child wounding a father with their rejection:

> I thought
> how I would set you among my children,
> and give you a pleasant land,
> the most beautiful heritage of all the nations.
> And I thought you would call me, My Father,
> and would not turn from following me. (3:19)

Despite all this, however, there remains throughout the Old Testament a certain reserve about the father metaphor for God.[10] There are nearly half a million words in the Hebrew Bible, yet God is only portrayed as a father some fifteen times.[11] It is almost as if these rare instances of the God of Israel being called (or calling Himself) "father" are placeholders, awaiting some unforeseen future revelation that will cause them to take on a new resonance.

When we turn to the New Testament, we immediately notice: gone is the reserve of the Old Testament when it comes to calling God "Father." If you were to tally how many times Jesus uses that name for God, the total would reach approximately 65 by the time you finished the Gospel of Luke and over 170 by the time you reached the end of the Gospel of John. Clearly, something new and surprising is afoot.

Jesus claims on several occasions in the Gospels to enjoy an unprecedented intimacy with God, and in these moments His calling God "Father" is especially prominent. "All things have been handed over to me by my Father; and no one knows the Son except the Father, and no one knows the Father except the Son and anyone to whom the Son chooses to reveal him," Jesus says (Matt 11:27). In the Gospel of John, Jesus' language is even stronger: "The Father and I are one" (10:30). And then, in the intimacy of prayer, on the eve of His crucifixion, Jesus exclaims, "So now, Father, glorify me in your own presence with the glory that I had in your presence before the world existed" (John 17:5). It took the church long centuries to plumb the implications of these cryptic words. Eventually, however, their significance could not be denied. What Jesus obliquely indicated in parables and symbolic gestures, the church has come to confess in clear, convicted prose.

From and to all eternity, God is one—but not in such a way that God is solitary. That's what Christians confess when they recite the Nicene Creed. Jesus Christ, the only Son of God, is "eternally begotten of the Father, God from God, Light from Light, true God from true God, begotten, not made, of one Being with the Father." The God Christians worship has no rivals but nor is He, for that reason, impersonal. Unfathomably, God exists *in* and *as* relationship. God the Father has a Son, whom He "begets"—here the creed uses the normal, if slightly archaic, word for human procreation. But this "begetting," this birthing, of the Father's Son does not happen in the way that human births do. It isn't physical, and it doesn't happen at any datable moment: contrary to an early Christian heresy, there was never a time when the Son was not. The Son's being begotten from His Father is, as the creed insists, eternal. Before and beyond all worlds (our time-bound language reaches its limits here), God is born from God but in such a way that there is only one God.[12] And as Father and Son fill and possess each other with something like sheer, radiant bliss, they do so in the love and delight of the Holy Spirit, who, like the Father and the Son, is eternal, without beginning or end, but who also—we reach the limits of language—is breathed out and given identity, we might say, by the Father and the Son together.

This is the ultimate origin of Jesus' teaching that God is Father. God has never *not* been the Father. His Son has never *not* been the Son. And their mutual love, the Spirit, has never begun nor ever ceased to bind them together in unbreakable communion. This mystery is part of what Jesus starts to disclose when He instructs His disciples to call God "Father."

T he first words of the Lord's Prayer, then—"Our Father in heaven"—are remarkable because Jesus calls God "Father," expressing a breathtaking intimacy with the One who had rescued Israel from Egypt. Those first words of the prayer are even more remarkable because with them, *we* are invited to address God in the same way that Jesus does. God is Father eternally, and Israel, too, in its memory of God's saving acts on its behalf, had known God by that name. But Jesus' words—His use of the plural possessive pronoun "our" is the key—beckon us to take our place alongside Him, looking up to Him as our older brother (Heb 2:10–18), entering into, partaking in, and emulating His relationship to God. For Him, that relationship has always been. He has never *not* enjoyed the privilege of communion with His Father. But for us, even those of us who have been born into God's covenant people, that relationship happens by enticement, as we are wooed into a new redemptive closeness with God through Jesus.[13] As Karl Barth puts it,

Jesus Christ, who is the Son of God, who has made himself our brother and makes us his brothers and sisters … takes us with him in order to associate us with himself, to place us beside him so that we may live and act as his family and as the members of his body. … Jesus Christ invites us, commands us, and allows us to speak with him to God, to pray with him his own prayer, to be united with him in the Lord's Prayer. Therefore he invites us to adore God, pray to God, and praise God with one mouth and one soul, with him, united to him.[14]

Barth is building on what St. Paul wrote shortly after Jesus' resurrection. Paul insists that Christians are those who have the boldness—there's that word again—to take on their lips Jesus' own address to God. We "receive adoption as children. And because you are children, God has sent the Spirit of His Son into our hearts, crying, 'Abba! Father!' " (Gal 4:5–6). Later, in his powerful Letter to the Romans, Paul would write similarly: "When we cry, 'Abba! Father!' it is that very Spirit bearing witness with our spirit that we are children of God" (8:15–16). We are tagalongs, you might say, taking advantage of the closeness Jesus enjoys with His Father. As the prophet Zechariah long ago predicted, people "from nations of every language shall take hold of a Jew, grasping his garment and saying, 'Let us go with you, for we have heard that God is with you' " (8:23). Indeed, God is with Jesus, and we do grasp our older brother's garment, begging Him to take us with Him to the Father. And He does.

What does it mean that Jesus tells us to pray to our Father "in heaven"? Heaven, as the Bible describes it, is not a far-off place in some distant galaxy. It is not a place at all in the sense we usually use that term, which makes it hard to talk about for people who cannot imagine existing without taking up space. Rather, "heaven" is a word that allows us to speak about God's nearness and availability without pinning Him down to a specific geographical address. Because God's life is not bodily, He is not limited by the categories of time and space that mark our human existence. God is not part of "the metaphysical furniture of the universe."[15] The earliest version of the Lord's Prayer, the one that goes back to Jesus himself, probably didn't have the phrase "in heaven." Luke's version says simply, "Father, hallowed be your name" (11:2). But Matthew adds it, perhaps in order to ward off any misunderstanding that God is a creaturely Father. Jesus' God is defined "over and against father gods, gods who beget the world."[16] The One whom Jesus calls "Father" is a *heavenly*, not an *earthly*, Father. As usual, it may be that the poet says it best:

> Our Father, You who dwell within the heavens—
> but are not circumscribed by them.[17]

Before we leave the opening address of the Lord's Prayer, we should pause to reflect on how, millennia after Jesus first bequeathed it to His followers, this prayer has become difficult for some of us to pray in ways that Jesus' first disciples could never have foreseen. Calling God "Father" is painful for many believers today because a long history of patriarchy (a social system—the only one most of us have ever known—in which men wield primary power and privilege) and fatherly abuse have robbed the term of much of its intended comfort. Feminist theologians have pointed out that we can easily toggle between thinking that God is beyond gender, but we call Him "Father" because that is what the Bible authorizes, and thinking that we call God "Father" because God *is* male. The former is what Christianity has always taught, but the latter is what many Christians seem to *hear*. And that, feminist thinkers rightly warn us, is dangerous.

Can anything be said in response to this? Other than lamenting and redoubling our commitment to work for social justice, Christians should also regularly reflect on and preach about how God's fatherhood must always and only be understood through His unity with His self-giving Son. Any picture of God as "Father" that leads us to think in terms of domination and cruelty rather than of humble service and unending love is not a true understanding of the God and Father of our Lord Jesus Christ, "who loved [us] and gave himself for [us]" (Gal 2:20).

Theologian Sarah Coakley has insisted that feminists not only *can* but *must* call God "Father" in order to help the church see that patriarchal interpretations of God's fatherhood aren't at all the best readings of what the Lord's Prayer is about. By adhering tenaciously to the conviction that "the *true* meaning of 'Father' is to be found in the Trinity," Christian feminists today may, through praying the Lord's Prayer, teach the rest of us why it isn't a charter for male domination.[18]

HALLOWED BE YOUR NAME

"HALLOWED BE YOUR NAME"

e are used to thinking of the ancient Greek and Romans gods by their names: Apollo, Dionysus, and so on. Their personalities—and hair-trigger tempers—are vivid and reliably tempestuous. Unlike them, Israel's God seems elusive, even inscrutable. Erich Auerbach, reflecting on the story in Genesis in which God comes to the patriarch Abraham and asks the unthinkable of him, notices the strangeness of God of the Bible by comparison with the Greek deities:

> He does not come, like Zeus or Poseidon, from the Aethiopians, where he has been enjoying a sacrificial feast. Nor are we told anything of his reasons for tempting Abraham so terribly. He has not, like Zeus, discussed them in set speeches with other gods gathered in council

> ... unexpected and mysterious, he enters the scene from
> some unknown height or depth and calls: Abraham![19]

To put it bluntly, the God of the Bible is beyond our categories of comprehension.

Despite His distance from the likes of Zeus or Apollo, Israel's God also has a personal name that He discloses to human beings. Near the beginning of the book of Exodus, we find this exchange between God and Moses, on the eve of Moses' journey back to Egypt to reunite with his ancestral people and lead them to freedom:

> Moses said to God, "If I come to the Israelites and say
> to them, 'The God of your ancestors has sent me to you,'
> and they ask me, 'What is his name?' what shall I say to
> them?" God said to Moses, "I AM WHO I AM." He said
> further, "Thus you shall say to the Israelites, 'I AM has
> sent me to you.' " God also said to Moses, "Thus you
> shall say to the Israelites, 'The LORD, the God of your
> ancestors, the God of Abraham, the God of Isaac, and
> the God of Jacob, has sent me to you':
>
> > This is my name forever,
> > and this my title for all generations. (Exod 3:13–15)

This English translation makes it hard to see, but the God of Israel's proper name lies behind "LORD," that word usually printed in all-capital letters in English Bibles. It is sometimes written out as "Yahweh" (or, in some older versions, "Jehovah"). Following ancient Jewish custom, English Bibles do not print this holy name, instead substituting a title, "Lord" (meaning "Master" or "Sovereign").

The divine name is a sort of pun. Its four Hebrew letters—*yod, heh, waw, heh* (Hebrew has no vowels)—are almost the same letters used in the earlier mysterious sentence, "I AM WHO I AM." But even more noteworthy is that this "name" of God doesn't seem to clarify much of anything about God's character or personality. According to Pope Benedict XVI, it is, paradoxically, "a name and a non-name at one and the same time."[20] In some mysterious way, God seems to be saying to Moses, "You may call Me by name, but do not make the mistake of thinking that you thereby *comprehend* Me. I am *free* to be Who I will be. My name means … I exist."

God's name, in other words, signifies His sheer transcendence—He is not like other gods, much less a mortal creature. Yet equally, it underscores His immanence—His nearness and availability to those who call out to Him. As one Jewish commentator put it, "God's pronouncement of His own Name indicates that the Divine Personality can be known only to the extent that God chooses to reveal His Self, and it can be truly characterized only in terms of itself, and not by analogy with something else."[21] God is God, with or without us. God doesn't need our assistance or support; rather, God gives us our existence. But, at the same time, God chooses not to be God without us. He offers His name to Moses. God makes a covenant with the people of Israel and promises to answer when they call. God lets Himself be known.

T hroughout the Old Testament, God is concerned that His name not be misunderstood. What would other nations think if the Lord, who had given Israel permission to call Him by name, suddenly reneged on His commitment to them? "For my name's sake I defer my anger," God says through the prophet Isaiah, "for the sake of my praise I restrain it for you, so that I may not cut you off" (Isa 48:9). God is acting to preserve His reputation: "For my own sake, for my own sake, I do it, for why should my name be profaned? My glory I will not give to another" (Isa 48:11).

So it comes as a complete shock when, centuries later, God *does* give His name to another. That gift is described by St. Paul:

> Therefore God also highly exalted [Christ Jesus]
>> and gave him the name
>> that is above every name. (Phil 2:9)

From henceforth, after Jesus' resurrection from the dead, people will call Him by the name of "Lord"—the same name that God had given to the people of Israel to call *Him* by. How this unimaginable gift could be given was one of the most unsettling and exciting mysteries that the earliest Christians had to ponder.

But the plot thickens even more. Elsewhere in his letters to young churches, Paul also names the quickening, empowering, gracious presence of God moving among believers—God's own Spirit—with the same personal name. "Now the Lord of whom [the book of Exodus] speaks is the Spirit" (2 Cor 3:17 REB). The name with which God named Himself to Moses—the same name that God handed over to Jesus as a crowning honor after Jesus' shameful death and resurrection—is also the name of the Spirit at work in the churches.

The only way this unthinkable trifold sharing of the one, holy divine name is conceivable is if Jesus and His—God's—Spirit are united to God in such a way that their mutual sharing of the same name isn't really "sharing," as we think of it, at all. Jesus and the Spirit must be so internal to God's identity, God's own life, that they are rightly called by the name of God. In giving the Son and the Spirit His name, the Father identifies Himself with Jesus Christ and the Holy Spirit in the most intimate way possible.[22] The Father says, in effect, "This is my Son. He, together with the Holy Spirit, is one with me. Listen to him" (see Matt 3:17; 17:5). It's no surprise, then—though it is breathtaking—when the Gospel of Matthew ends with a mention of a singular *name*: "the name of the Father and of the Son and of the Holy Spirit" (28:19).

T he word "hallow" means to "honor" or "make uncommon"—to "make something special," as we might say in contemporary English. According to Simone Weil, when we ask God to "hallow" His name, "we are asking for something that *exists* eternally, with full and complete reality, so that we can neither increase nor diminish it, even by an infinitesimal fraction."[23] God's name *is already* uncommon, regardless of whether we acknowledge it or not.

That name has been uttered in love by the Father, His Son, and their Spirit from before all worlds. To pray for God's name to be hallowed is to ask God to preserve and display this mysteriously radiant reality. It is to ask God to keep before the eyes of the world this drama of divine majesty and mercy so that we can continue to speak it back to God in worship and cling to it in times of desperation.

We may think, for instance, of a Christian like Polycarp, one of the earliest Christian martyrs. In the second century, faced with the demand that he hallow the emperor of Rome as "Lord" and "Savior," Polycarp refused and said, "For eighty-six years I have been serving [Jesus Christ], and he has done me no wrong. Indeed how can I blaspheme my king who saved me?"[24] Closer to home, we may think of a Christian like Kevin Harris formerly of the Marin Foundation, who, when he was living in Chicago's Boystown neighborhood, grew concerned about the damage done when his fellow Christians led many lesbian and gay people to believe that God's message for them was only one of judgment. The Marin Foundation started the "I'm Sorry" campaign, in which Christians attended LGBT pride parades and apologized for not communicating more clearly the message of God's love and mercy for all sinners without exception.[25] The Marin Foundation's initiative might be seen as protecting God's name—upholding God's reputation by acting in ways that emphasize His love.

Through costly actions like these, Christians show their reverence for the divine name that is always and already holy. Clifton Black connects God's own hallowing of His name and our reverencing it in response: "God's self-consecration kindles in us the yearning to revere the Almighty as God alone deserves."[26] As we meditate on God's eternal holiness, we may begin to ask ourselves: What words and actions on our part are fitting complements to this reality?

YOUR KINGDOM COME

"YOUR KINGDOM COME"

 n contemporary English, the word "kingdom" primarily denotes a place. A king's kingdom is the land over which he rules. But when Mark the Evangelist wanted to sum up the way Jesus started His earthly ministry, he used these words:

> Now after John was arrested, Jesus came to Galilee, proclaiming the good news of God, and saying, "The time is fulfilled, and the kingdom of God has come near; repent, and believe in the good news." (1:14–15)

The Greek word that Mark and the other Gospel writers use to summarize Jesus' message—*basileia*—is probably better translated with a word that indicates *activity*. A word like "rule," "reign," or even "kingship" is closer to the original meaning of *basileia*—which means that when Jesus says "the kingdom of

God has come near," He is proclaiming that God is asserting His rule in the world in and through Jesus' ministry. Jesus is heralding the fact that God—like a king who has been abroad and absent from his native land—finally is returning to take back His throne. Jesus is announcing a sort of re-coronation. The God we might have thought was silent, never to be heard from again, is back on the scene and ready to rule.

But what *kind* of rule will it be? Coronations can be terrifying. The enthronement of a new king or leader can make one queasy with dread. If you've never had to fear when a new prime minister, president, or monarch comes into power, then you have lived a life of rare privilege. For many people in the world—throughout history and also presently, even in the modern West—the passing of power to a new ruler is a matter of gnawing anxiety.

A scene from the end of *The Godfather*—one of the most haunting pieces of cinema I've ever seen—captures this fear well. The protagonist, Michael Corleone, stands near the baptismal font in an ornate Catholic church for his nephew's christening. As the camera lingers on his stoic facial expression and elegant suit, the scene cuts to a series of assassinations that Michael has orchestrated, which are happening at the very same time as the service of baptism. It turns out that Michael has arranged to become the kingpin of the New York mob, and he is ascending to his throne by means of a bloodbath. The cost of his rule is the death of anyone who stands in his way. The agonizing, devastating final scene of the film shows him being crowned, as it were, as "Don Corleone"—the new monarch of terror.

This fictional story is haunting enough, but similar stories happen in real life all the time. Dictators trample on human dignity to ascend their thrones. Terrorists seize the reins of power. Evil overlords who care nothing for the poor or the sick take control of governments and kingdoms, and the citizens consequently fear for their lives. Coronations, for much of the world, are occasions of uncertainty, worry, and alarm.

Perhaps that same worry and alarm was stirred up in the hearts of Jesus' hearers when He preached. His message about God's reign would have conjured up all the churning emotions that coronations usually conjure up: the trembling uncertainty about how severe the new king's reign would be, the nagging apprehension that the king might demand of them what they aren't able to give, the dread of what wars the king might lead them into. This is the way things go with kings in our world. Perhaps Jesus' hearers would have remembered the words of the prophet Samuel:

> These will be the ways of the king who will reign over you: he will take your sons and appoint them to his chariots and to be his horsemen, and to run before his chariots; and he will appoint for himself commanders of thousands and commanders of fifties, and some to plow his ground and to reap his harvest, and to make his implements of war and the equipment of his chariots.

He will take your daughters to be perfumers and cooks and bakers. He will take the best of your fields and vineyards and olive orchards and give them to his courtiers. He will take one-tenth of your grain and of your vineyards and give it to his officers and his courtiers. He will take your male and female slaves, and the best of your cattle and donkeys, and put them to his work. He will take one-tenth of your flocks, and you shall be his slaves. And in that day you will cry out because of your king. (1 Sam 8:11–18)

The world of first-century Judea was sadly familiar with this sort of kingly script. The Jews of Palestine were used to ambitious would-be rulers rising through the ranks by means of betrayal and intrigue and nighttime assassinations. They were familiar with the story of Julius Caesar's stabbing. They knew the way that plot unfolds.

But God's now-arriving rule doesn't follow the usual pattern, according to Jesus. God's reign spells liberation for Israel, not coercion. God taking up His crown means the dawning of a new era of deliverance, not domination. When Jesus wants to point His hearers to the telltale signs of God's kingship bursting onto the scene, He says things like this: "But if it is by the finger of God that I cast out the demons, then the kingdom of God has come to you" (Luke 11:20). Where you see people being delivered from oppression, in other words, *there* you see God's reign in action. Jesus made His followers into emissaries of God's saving rule; "he sent them out to proclaim the kingdom of God and to heal" (Luke 9:2). Where you see healing and the restoration of what sin and death have disfigured, *there* you see God's kingship displayed.

That is what Jesus teaches His followers to cry out for: "Your kingdom come" means "Father, make Your healing reign more and more tangible and visible in our world. Let Your rule assert itself ever more concretely in the places where sickness and evil still seem to have the upper hand."

Jesus also teaches His followers to pray "Your kingdom come" because—we must not evade this uncomfortable truth—God's rule is not yet visible in the way we long for it to be. God's reign, Jesus says,

> is like a mustard seed, which, when sown upon the ground, is the smallest of all the seeds on earth; yet when it is sown it grows up and becomes the greatest of all shrubs, and puts forth large branches, so that the birds of the air can make nests in its shade. (Mark 4:31–32)

Or, as He puts it in another place, "The kingdom of heaven is like yeast that a woman took and mixed in with three measures of flour until all of it was leavened" (Matt 13:33). God's rule is breaking into the world in Jesus' ministry—but not in such a way that it can be readily identified by the unaided human eye. We can discern it by faith, but we don't yet *see* it in the way that we will someday.

One illustration that modern Bible interpreters use to describe the mysterious already-but-not-yet nature of God's reign is the distinction between "D-Day," the operation whereby the Allied forces in World War II secured a foothold in France in 1944, and "V-E Day," or "Victory in Europe Day," which came some eleven months later when Nazi Germany offered its unconditional surrender.[27] Historians looking back now recognize that the war was effectively won when the Allies landed on Normandy's beaches. The D-Day invasion hearkened the end of the Nazi regime, even though the death camps kept running and many more lives of combatants and civilians alike were lost before Germany's surrender in May of the following year.

It's as though we live between two similarly momentous days. We look backward to the life, death, and resurrection of Jesus as the moment when God's rule showed itself to be unconquerable—theological D-Day, we might call it. In a very real way, God's conquest of His rebellious world was achieved when His Son left His tomb behind on Easter morning. Yet suffering continues, and we go on longing for an end that isn't yet public and universal. In this time between the times, as we await Christ's coming in glory, we who have caught the vision of the way the war will end, we "who have the first fruits of the Spirit, groan inwardly while we wait for adoption, the redemption of our bodies" (Rom 8:23). We know that God will one day do for us and for His whole creation what He did for Jesus in raising Him from the dead, but for now, in the meantime, we weep and wait. And that is why we continue to pray, "Your kingdom come," meaning, "Father, let us see, in the present, more and more signs that the war You have won against the powers that corrupt and enslave Your world is nearing its consummation. Give us more tangible previews of that great day when death will be swallowed up in victory. Help us see that Jesus' resurrection isn't just a one-off event but will sweep us along in its wake so that we will share in His transformation."

"We are waiting," says Karl Barth, "until Easter becomes for the world a general event."[28]

YOUR WILL BE DONE
ON EARTH AS IN HEAVEN

"YOUR WILL BE DONE ON EARTH AS IN HEAVEN"

In the time it has taken me to compose this sentence, two children have died from malaria, around a dozen children under the age of five have passed away from hunger, and over one hundred babies around the world have been killed in the womb. It reminds me of a line from the end of *The Private Patient* by P. D. James: "If the screams of all earth's living creatures were one scream of pain, surely it would shake the stars."[29] The image is haunting—a terrible choir of pain, God's ears bombarded by the screams of agony of His creation.

If God's own life consists of the sheer bliss of love shared by Father, Son, and Spirit, the mismatch between that reality and all these horrors is unconscionable—and the third petition of the Lord's Prayer forces us to confront that. When we pray, "Your will be done, on earth as in heaven," we are aware of how God's will is *not* being done in our world. We are asking God to overcome this contradiction, to act in such a way that life on earth increasingly resembles the peaceable and joyous life of God, of heaven.

In petitionary prayer, we set ourselves against what seems "normal." If a world filled with cancer, AIDS, sex slavery, rapacious greed, and toxic waste seems to us like "just the way things are," then petitionary prayer invites us to imagine a different world—the world as God meant it to be and will ultimately make it, a world in which those things are profoundly abnormal. To pray "Your will be done" is to adopt an appropriate distress over the world as it exists now and to hold on to the conviction that God will even now begin to change the world. As theologian David Wells puts it,

> Petitionary prayer only flourishes where there is a two-fold belief: first, that God's name is hallowed too irregularly, His kingdom has come too little, and His will is done too infrequently; second, that God Himself can change this situation. Petitionary prayer, therefore, is the expression of the hope that life as we meet it, on the one hand, *can* be otherwise and, on the other hand, that it *ought* to be otherwise. ... To pray declares that God and His world are at cross-purposes.[30]

So as we pray for God's reign to become more fully visible, as we ask for God's perfect heavenly wholeness to come on earth as well, we are asking for the aftershocks of the fall to be quieted, declaring, "Let your glory be over all the earth" (Ps 57:5). We are, in effect, taking our stand against the world as it is now and asking for more and more foretastes of the world as it will be when the kingdom of God is finally consummated.[31]

But how does that happen? How does God respond to our asking for His will to be done on earth as in heaven? In order to answer that question, once again we have to see how Jesus demonstrates in His own life what it means to pray His prayer.

On the eve of His crucifixion, Jesus prays in the way He had earlier instructed His disciples to pray: "My Father, if it is possible, let this cup pass from me; yet not what I want but what you want. ... My Father, if this cannot pass unless I drink it, your will be done" (Matt 26:39, 42). In Greek, the wording of the Lord's Prayer and the wording of Jesus' anguished cry in the garden are identical (compare Matt 6:10 with 26:39, 42). And the way that prayer is answered, of course—the way the Father's will comes to be done on earth, in that hour—is that Jesus is *not* rescued from His fate. He is arrested, tried, bound, scourged, and crucified. This doesn't look like the peace of heaven dispelling the darkness of the earth so much as the reverse.

What should we make of that? More pointedly, how ought Jesus' prayer in Gethsemane to shape our understanding of

God's will coming to be done on earth? Just so: in a world marked by sin and death, for the will of God—the wholeness, life, and love of God—to take root on earth requires the vanquishing of that sin and death. It won't do to say that God is only found in moments of obvious health, beauty, and joy. God must also be at work in suffering, in darkness, in torment, because the triumph of God's love can be assured only if God confronts the horror we've made of the world, bears it, and removes it. Only if the will of God mysteriously includes Jesus' death on a cross can the will of God be guaranteed. All other solutions would be mere Band-Aids, putting off the inevitable confrontation by papering over it. If the heavenly will of God is to be enacted on a sin-scorched earth, then it must also be the will of God for Jesus to enter fully into the pain of that earth. The way to God's will being done lies *through* Jesus' suffering, not through its avoidance. Only by entering into and overcoming the world's evil can Jesus usher in the healing we pray for.

The will of God that is done in heaven is clearly the perfect, eternal love of Father, Son, and Spirit, unmarred by any suffering or dying. What is less intuitive—but what Gethsemane and, later, Calvary force us to notice—is that the will of God is also the way of the incarnate Lord into the far country of *our* suffering and dying, where He is mocked, spit upon, strung up, and left to suffocate. *That* is what it looks like for the will of God to be done on earth as it is in heaven because *that* is the only way our earth can be saved.

P erhaps here is as good a place as any to pause and ask what we mean when we say that *we* petition *God*. If the Christian tradition is right to call God unchanging, then what sense does it make to ask God to act in accord with our prayers? Is it the case that our asking for God's kingdom to come and will to be done on earth is what moves God to usher in the kingdom and assert His will?

Martin Luther was one of many Christians who saw clearly that the point of petitionary prayer is not to try to convince God to do something He otherwise would not do. Luther insisted that instead, asking for God's kingdom and will to be made manifest—which they would be, regardless of our efforts—is about stretching our hearts so that we may learn to desire truer, greater realities. As C. S. Lewis says in the stage play and film *Shadowlands*, "I pray because I can't help myself. I pray because I'm helpless. I pray because the need flows out of me all the time, waking and sleeping. It doesn't change God. It changes me."[32]

GIVE US TODAY
OUR DAILY BREAD

"GIVE US TODAY OUR DAILY BREAD"

fter the Reformer Martin Luther died, his friends who came to his room to remove his corpse found a note he had scrawled sometime in his final days: "We are beggars, that is true."[33]

With those scribbled phrases, Luther summed up his own hard-won theological perspective on what it means to be a human being: we are all utterly dependent on divine grace alone. Our supposed merits are insufficient to win us any favor with God. But Luther's final sentence also expresses one of the chief themes of the Lord's Prayer: far from being self-sustaining, we are needy creatures, reliant on energy from a source outside ourselves if we are to go on living. We are like beggars, whose only hope for food and shelter is the compassion of Another.

When Jesus teaches us to pray "Give us today our daily bread," He is first of all training us to see ourselves in a certain way in relation to God. To the surprise of His status-conscious disciples, He insists, "Truly I tell you, unless you change and become like children, you will never enter the kingdom of heaven" (Matt 18:3). If there is one fact that is obvious about children, it is their *dependence*. Unless a parent or guardian provides milk for a baby, the infant will die. According to Jesus, that remains our true condition into our adulthood, whether we are conscious of it or not. Were God to withdraw His nourishment from us, we would not just slowly shrivel but immediately cease to exist.

A professor of mine described the Christian doctrines of creation and divine providence with the analogy of a plugged-in TV. If someone were to unplug the TV's cord, it isn't the case that the characters on screen would gradually fade, their words and gestures growing more and more sluggish until the screen went dark altogether. Rather, as soon as the TV's connection to its source of power is cut off, the images cease to flicker. The TV has no electricity of its own; it projects its images only by constant connection to its electrical feed. We likewise are dependent on God's *continual* "upholding all things by the word of his power" (Heb 1:3 KJV). That's why the Lord's Prayer includes the word "today." It is not enough for God to kick-start the process of sustaining human beings and then sit back like a parent retreating into a book while the children race off to attempt some task or play by themselves. On the contrary, we rely on God's provision each moment of our lives.

And we shouldn't overlook the fact that Jesus teaches us to request that provision. Nineteenth-century Anglican priest and theologian F. D. Maurice recommended that wealthy, well-fed Christians in particular should ponder this petition during Lent, the forty days leading up to Easter during which many believers fast from certain luxuries, culinary or otherwise. Some Christians, says Maurice,

> are apt to mock God when they speak these solemn words ["Give us today our daily bread"], apt to take food and every other blessing as if it were their right of which no power in heaven or earth except by sheer injustice can deprive them. Something which shall tell them of dependence, some secret reminiscence, insignificant to others, that all things are not their own; some hint that there are a few million creatures of their flesh and blood who cannot call any of these things their own, is needful for them.[34]

Those well-nourished Christians who stop eating meat during Lent, says Maurice, "are desiring to recollect that it is a good which He *bestows*."[35] They are trying, in other words, to pray "Give us today our daily bread" with more sincere humility, recognizing that God does not owe them food but may nonetheless be pleased to supply it. Voluntarily going without bread for a while will help you realize how much you need it and how little power you yourself have to guarantee that you'll always have it.

Jesus himself models the posture of dependence on God that He commends to His followers. (This is our recurring theme. As Karl Barth puts it, "The Commander ... embodies the command."[36]) Each petition of the Lord's Prayer is a window onto Jesus' character and actions before it is instruction for us.

After being baptized in the Jordan River in solidarity with repentant Israel and while abstaining from food in the wilderness before launching His public ministry, Jesus experienced the gnaw of hunger and knew what it meant to depend on God for His survival. "He ate nothing at all during those days, and when they were over, he was famished," says Luke's Gospel (4:2). While His stomach was empty, the devil appeared to Jesus and proposed that He perform a miracle of converting desert rocks into warm loaves, but Jesus spurned the suggestion. "It is written, 'One does not live by bread alone,' " He replied, invoking the story of God supplying the Israelites with manna (Luke 4:4, quoting Deut 8:3). Refusing to assume the rebel posture of self-reliance, Jesus told His tempter that He would wait for His Father to give Him bread on His own terms.

This was, after all, the point of the story that Jesus alluded to. Having escaped slavery in Egypt, the people of Israel found themselves tempted again and again to forget their sheer dependence on God for their freedom. No sooner had they made it through the middle of the sea without so much as getting their feet damp than they built an altar to a self-made god. As soon as they remembered the abundance they had left behind, they were inclined to perceive God as having cheated them. This is why God directly—without waiting for the process of seed-ing, harvesting, threshing, and baking to produce bread—gave manna to the Israelites. According to the passage Jesus quoted, Moses instructs the people: "He humbled you by letting you hunger, then by feeding you with manna, with which neither you nor your ancestors were acquainted, in order to make you understand that one does not live by bread alone, but by every word that comes from the mouth of the LORD." Through His obedience, Jesus enacts His own prayer. He demonstrates what it looks like to trust in the manna-giving God, the One He called "Father."

I n John 6, Jesus once again talks about the Old Testament story of manna in the wilderness. Disputing with Him, the religious leaders of Judea challenge Jesus to perform some certi-fying gesture: "What sign are you going to give us then, so that we may see it and believe you?" They go on (helpfully, they must suppose) to suggest the kind of thing they have in mind for Jesus to do: "Our ancestors ate the manna in the wilderness; as it is written, 'He gave them bread from heaven to eat.' " They seem to say that Jesus should act like Moses, calling down food from the skies and causing water to gush out of rocks.

Mysteriously, though, when He answers them, Jesus leaps from the story His opponents cite, a story of God's miraculous care in the past, to the immediate present: "Very truly, I tell you, it was not Moses who gave you the bread from heaven, but it is my Father who gives you the true bread from heaven. For the bread of God is that which comes down from heaven and gives life to the world" (John 6:30, 31, 32–33). And then, in case they miss the point, He spells out what He means:

> I am the bread of life. Your ancestors ate the manna in the wilderness, and they died. ... I am the living bread that came down from heaven. Whoever eats of this bread will live forever; and the bread that I will give for the life of the world is my flesh. (John 6:48–51)

Manna is sustaining only for so long, Jesus insists. Bread can keep human beings alive but not for forever. For eternal life, stronger, more substantial bread is needed—and that bread is His own life, offered for human consumption. Jesus promises, "Those who eat my flesh and drink my blood have eternal life, and I will raise them up on the last day; for my flesh is true food and my blood is true drink" (John 6:54–55).

When we come back to the Lord's Prayer after hearing Jesus' discourse on the bread of life and His flesh given to the world for eating, it becomes hard not to see Jesus *Himself* as the daily bread He encourages us to pray for. In her meditations on the Lord's Prayer, Simone Weil says simply, "Christ is our bread."[37] This explains why the churches of both the East and West pray the Lord's Prayer just before the distribution of Communion. The priest consecrates the bread and wine, asking the Holy Spirit to sanctify them so that they might be the body and blood of Christ for the faithful. As worshipers go up to receive these gifts, they receive at the same time the answer to their prayer moments earlier: "Give us today our daily bread."

In the Eucharist, Jesus puts Himself in our hands so we know exactly where to find Him.[38] In that moment, we don't have to wonder whether God is for us. We *know* He is because we've just tasted His provision. He gives us His Son—His life-giving flesh.

FORGIVE US OUR SINS AS WE FORGIVE THOSE WHO SIN AGAINST US

"FORGIVE US OUR SINS AS WE FORGIVE THOSE WHO SIN AGAINST US"

One of my friends tells a story about taking his uncle to an Episcopal church for the first time. Each Sunday, prior to receiving Communion, worshipers in Episcopal churches say these words: "Most merciful God, we confess that we have sinned against you in thought, word, and deed ..." My friend's uncle, seeing those words in the prayer book, squirmed uncomfortably. Later, he told my friend: "Should we really expect *everyone* to confess that they've sinned that week? That's what having a prayer of confession suggests—that every single one of us needs to acknowledge some sin. But what about those Christians who have gained victory over sin already? Surely they shouldn't be forced to confess what isn't true."

Without entering into the complicated history of ideas like "victorious Christian living" or "entire sanctification," I am struck by what my friend's uncle saw so clearly. By having a confession of sins as part of the church's regular liturgy, the Episcopal Church is indeed making the assumption that everyone attending church that morning needs to make that confession. Where I differ from my friend's uncle is in thinking that this practice, far from being problematic, simply expands on what Jesus encouraged in the church when He gave the Lord's Prayer to His disciples. "Pray then in this way," He said to His followers—all of them—who had gathered on the hillside to hear His sermon (Matt 6:9). Included were these words: "Forgive us our sins as we forgive those who sin against us."

Elsewhere in the New Testament, we're warned of the danger of pretending that we're somehow above the need for regular forgiveness. The First Letter of John imagines that some of its hearers might be deluded about their complicity in evil prior to their baptism: "If we say that we have not sinned, we make [God] a liar, and his word is not in us" (1 John 1:10). But a more subtle danger lurks alongside this one. Other believers, honest about their prior guilt and confident of their new status as God's children, may claim present innocence while admitting to past failures. But the apostle is equally insistent that this won't do. "If we say that we have no sin," 1 John says, changing the verb tense, "we deceive ourselves, and the truth is not in us" (1:8). Whatever the Epistle of 1 Peter means when it says that "whoever has suffered in the flesh has finished with sin" (4:1), it shouldn't be read as inviting us to think of ourselves as beyond the need for daily mercy and pardon. The Articles of Religion that helped form the theology of Anglican churches speaks about sin like a disease that is passed on genetically, one that even baptism does not heal all at once: "This infection of nature doth remain, yea in them that are regenerated."[39] It would seem that by encouraging His disciples to regularly say, "Forgive us our sins," Jesus is the ultimate originator of this unblinking view of human frailty.

The fact that we pray "Forgive us our sins" not just once at our baptism but again and again says something significant about the nature of sin. For many of us, the word "sin" conjures up childhood memories of stealing a cookie when we were told not to or of messages we heard in adolescence from youth pastors about the wickedness of certain kinds of sex. "Sin," we may think, is a word preachers use to try to inoculate us against the appeal of forbidden pleasures. And yet it would seem that Jesus expects even those who have been able to rise above certain bad habits, like stealing cookies or cheating on one's spouse, to go on praying, "Forgive us our sins." This suggests that what the Lord's Prayer is referring to is something deeper, wider, more pervasive, and intractable than individual peccadilloes or improvable behaviors. To return to the language of the liturgy, Jesus appears to be encouraging a view of sin as "what we have done and … what we have left undone."[40] It won't do to think of sin as something I've been able to rise above through sheer dint of hard work, while on the other hand, you are still mired in it. Nor is it sufficient for me to congratulate myself on having stolen no cookies or having had no illicit sex this past week and therefore count myself freed from the obligation on Sunday to pray the fifth petition of the Lord's Prayer.

Augustine of Hippo was someone who understood sin's true depths better than most. In order to illustrate why we all must think of ourselves as sinners, even if we've made enormous progress in developing habits of virtue and godliness, Augustine pointed to the heart of God's law, the command that Jesus described as the greatest: "You shall love the Lord your God with all your heart, and with all your soul, and with all your mind" (Matt 22:37, quoting Deut 6:5). It is certainly the case, Augustine admitted, that many Christians do love the Lord their God. But can any of us say that we love God with *all* our heart, with *all* our soul, with *all* our minds?[41] Like a relentless therapist, Augustine won't let us dissemble. Which one of us can say with a straight face that we are withholding none of our devotion and loyalty from God? And, in any case, even if we could say that, we still haven't reckoned with the second great commandment: "You shall love your neighbor as yourself" (Matt 22:39, quoting Lev 19:18). If by some miracle we were able to love God with the entirety of our being, experience demonstrates that even the best of us aren't able to love those around us with the same deference, understanding, and magnanimity that we reserve for ourselves. This is why the liturgy insists that we pray before each Eucharist: "We have not loved you with our whole heart. We have not loved our neighbors as ourselves. We are truly sorry, and we humbly repent."[42]

Once you adopt this deeper and darker view of human corruption, it becomes harder to hold on to any religious pride—and, by the same token, harder to look down on others as somehow worse off than yourself. We're circling around the Christian doctrine of original sin, vividly described by Francis Spufford as the conviction that committing actual murder is in the same family of actions as "telling a story at a dinner party at the expense of an absent mutual friend, a story which you know will cause pain when it gets back to them but you tell it anyway, because it's just very, very funny." One of these things may take a life, and the other may take a piece of a soul, but both are motivated by "a certain self-pleasing smirk," and in that way, both are devastating to both perpetrator and victim.[43] It's *that* which we're praying God to release us from when we ask, "Forgive us our sins."

One of the troubling things about the fifth petition of the Lord's Prayer is the way it seems to make God's forgiving us contingent on our forgiving others. That's at least how many Christians have interpreted the relationship between the two halves of the petition. "Forgive us our sins as we forgive those who sin against us" means, in many minds, "Forgive us our sins *because* we forgive those who sin against us." The Protestant

Reformers, especially, worried about the kind of spirituality that this interpretation promotes. In their experience, people who came to God with their supposedly virtuous actions and tried to use them as bartering chips to get God to dispense mercy were often secretly living in terror of God. If you approach God asking for forgiveness and supplying your own efforts at forgiving others as the basis for why God should grant your request, chances are you're a deeply fearful believer, expecting God to cast you out of sight if you don't display a worthy enough track record. Martin Luther was fond of pointing out if you think that your generosity toward others is somehow going to get you off the divine hook, then it isn't really generosity. Only actions that are motivated by love, rather than self-preservation, can be truly generous. If your need to bolster your own righteousness is your motivation for forgiving and serving other people, then your efforts at forgiveness and service are more about you than they are about the people you're supposedly interested in caring for.

But John Calvin suggests that there is another way to read the fifth petition of the Lord's Prayer. In the lovely exposition that he provides in book 3 of his *Institutes of the Christian Religion*, Calvin first points out the problem we've been discussing:

> We must note that this condition—that [God] "forgive us as we forgive our debtors" [Matt. 6:12]—is not added because by the forgiveness we grant others we deserve his forgiveness, as if [our forgiveness] indicated the cause of [God's forgiveness].[44]

Calvin had been gripped by the Pauline insight that God's forgiveness is never conditioned by our actions to say otherwise. On the contrary, we are made capable of forgiving others through God's having first forgiven us. The order is crucial. As Paul wrote, "Be kind to one another, tenderhearted, forgiving one another, as God in Christ has [already] forgiven you" (Eph 4:32).

So, says Calvin, we must look for another way to understand the Lord's Prayer:

> By this word the Lord intended partly to comfort the weakness of our faith. For he has added this as a sign to assure us he has granted forgiveness of sins to us just as surely as we are aware of having forgiven others, provided our hearts have been emptied and purged of all hatred, envy, and vengeance.[45]

In other words, Calvin says, Jesus isn't offering a *condition* for our receiving God's forgiveness so much as He is offering an *illustration* of what God's disposition toward us is really like. Think about the times when you have actually extended forgiveness to someone who hurt you. Remember the stirring in your gut when your spouse or your sibling brokenheartedly acknowledged the way they were in the wrong, the way they neglected you, humiliated you, or stabbed you in the back. Recall the surge of compassion that you experienced when you said out loud to them, "I forgive you. I don't hold this against you, and it's not going to keep me from continuing to love you."

That, says Calvin, is what Jesus wants you to hold in your mind as you pray to God to forgive you because God's forgiveness is *that* wonderful, only more so.

In Luke's Gospel, just after He offers the Lord's Prayer to His disciples, Jesus says:

> Is there anyone among you who, if your child asks for a fish, will give a snake instead of a fish? Or if the child asks for an egg, will give a scorpion? If you then, who are evil, know how to give good gifts to your children, how much more will the heavenly Father give the Holy Spirit to those who ask him! (Luke 11:11–13)

It may be that the so-called condition attached to the fifth petition of the Lord's Prayer means to say no more than this: "If you then, who are prone to nurse petty grudges, know how to extend forgiveness to your friends when the time comes, how much will your heavenly Father forgive you when you ask Him!"

In the liturgy, just before we pray the Lord's Prayer, we hear the words Jesus spoke on the night of His betrayal. Taking the chalice of wine in His hands, He said, "Drink this, all of you: This is my blood of the new covenant, which is shed for you and for many for the forgiveness of sins." A few moments later in the liturgy, we pray, "Forgive us our sins," and we know in that moment, because of Jesus, that God will.

SAVE US
FROM THE TIME OF TRIAL

"SAVE US FROM THE TIME OF TRIAL"

Pope Francis made headlines around the world when he suggested in a TV interview that it might be time to change the wording of the Lord's Prayer. Speaking of the sixth petition of the prayer, familiar to English speakers in the King James Version as "Lead us not into temptation," the pope said:

> It is not a good translation because it speaks of a God who induces temptation. I am the one who falls; it's not [God] pushing me into temptation to then see how I have fallen. A father doesn't do that, a father helps you to get up immediately. It's Satan who leads us into temptation, that's his department.[46]

On the one hand, the pope seemed to make a good point. In Christian theology, God is never understood as the origin of evil. James rules that out in no uncertain terms: "No one, when tempted, should say, 'I am being tempted by God'; for God cannot be tempted by evil and he himself tempts no one" (1:13). Human beings often project our own cruel or foolish inclinations onto God, imagining that God, like us, sometimes lures others into sin just for the fun or meanness of it. But the God we see in Jesus Christ isn't like that. God is the One who rescues us from sin, who makes us long for holiness and goodness—not the One who incites us to go against the grain of His loving will. James again: "One is tempted by one's own desire, being lured and enticed by it" (1:14). We aren't tempted by God.

And yet, on the other hand, the Bible does feature numerous stories in which God, like a metalsmith, applies pressure on His people to refine their faith and obedience, to make it stronger and more durable. The most famous example is the binding of Isaac, in which God subjects His covenant partner Abraham to the utmost test of loyalty: "After these things God tested Abraham. He said to him, 'Abraham!' And he said, 'Here I am.' He said, 'Take your son, your only son Isaac, whom you love, and go to the land of Moriah, and offer him there as a burnt offering on one of the mountains that I shall show you'" (Gen 22:1–2). Isaac, it turns out, is spared the knife, but not before his father's heart has been put through the furnace. Abraham's faith endures—"Now I know that you fear God, since you have not withheld your son, your only son, from me" (Gen 22:12)—but not because the Lord has exempted him from the ultimate trial.

God's testing is central to the way He relates to Israel in the Old Testament. At key junctures in Israel's life with God, God brings it about that His people are laid on the anvil. "Prove me, O LORD, and try me; test my heart and mind," prays the psalmist (26:2), and the Lord does. A story like Abraham's, being asked to offer up his beloved son Isaac to God, is one that invites us, too, to reflect on our own dark nights of the soul and to ask how God might be sifting our faith to uncover its mettle.[47] Whatever else the petition "Lead us not into temptation" means, it cannot mean that God will spare us the searing heat of the refiner's fire. When those moments come, we should be prepared to say with Shadrach, Meshach, and Abednego, "If our God whom we serve is able to deliver us from the furnace of blazing fire and out of your hand, O king, let him deliver us. But if not, be it known to you, O king, that we will not serve your gods" (Dan 3:17–18).

What, then, does it mean for us to petition God to save us from the time of trial? The best clue lies in following the occurrences of the word we translate as "temptation" or "trial" in English. The Greek word that lies behind these English words is *peirasmos*. The verbal form of it appears in the Gospel of Matthew just after Jesus has been baptized in the Jordan River. Like Israel emerging from their journey through the Red Sea, Jesus immediately goes into the wilderness. Matthew puts it this way: "Then Jesus was led up by the Spirit into the wilderness to be tempted by the devil" (4:1). At least two details are crucial for us to notice. First, we should observe that the Spirit of God doesn't prevent Jesus from facing temptation. On the contrary, the Spirit is the One who leads Jesus toward it. Like Job in the Old Testament, Jesus faces extreme testing precisely in and through God's providence. Far from being aloof or unaware as Jesus enters the wastelands of Judea to face His tempter, God arranges for His passage.

But, second, God is not the one doing the tempting. That is the devil's business. The Spirit may be the superintendent of the play, but He doesn't assume the role of the villain who appears on stage with Jesus.

The Greek word *peirasmos* shows up yet again in Matthew's Gospel toward the very end of the narrative. Just after Jesus has celebrated His final supper with His disciples, He and they depart for the garden of Gethsemane. When they arrive, Jesus exhorts His disciples, "Stay awake and pray that you may not come into the time of trial [*peirasmos*]" (26:41). Although the disciples may not know it, we know that this will be the darkest night of Jesus' life. All of human evil is converging on that garden, circling like a vulture above Jesus' head. Jesus says to His enemies, "This is your hour, and the power of darkness" (Luke 22:53). That "hour" ends with Jesus being arrested, to the shock of His disciples; later that night, facing an unjust trial; and, hours later, being nailed to a cross and left to suffer the curse of death.

At both the beginning and the end of His earthly ministry, Jesus faces the truest, deepest form of temptation or trial. He burrows into temptation's depths and breathes the suffocating atmosphere of trial as He prays in Gethsemane and, ultimately, dies on the cross. And He does it alone. As Hans Urs von Balthasar puts it, "Jesus prays *in* the *peirasmos*, whereas the disciples pray to be preserved *from* it."[48] The disciples may be there beside Jesus in the garden and, more distantly, on Calvary's hill, but they are not there in the furnace of temptation *with* Jesus. They are onlookers but not full participants. They witness Jesus' temptation and agony, but they do not—they cannot—bear it in the way that He does.

This should affect the way we pray this particular petition of the Lord's Prayer. We pray, "Save us from the time of trial" or "Lead us not into temptation," depending on the translation. Reading these words in the context of the entire gospel, we can see immediately that God intends to answer—has *already* answered—this prayer. We will be saved from the time of ultimate trial, sheltered from it and spared from ever experiencing its true horrors, because there is One who already has experienced those horrors in our place. Because Jesus was not saved from temptation, we are.

Whatever temptations God permits us to endure, we may be confident that they are never punitive. The New Testament does teach that believers will go through times of tribulation (and we can verify that teaching empirically: think of the persecuted church around the world today, illustrated horrifically by the Coptic martyrs beheaded in Libya in 2015 by ISIS operatives[49]). The First Letter of Peter warns us away from any shock at God's refusal to spare us such times: "Beloved, do not be surprised at the fiery ordeal [*peirasmos*] that is taking place among you to test you, as though something strange were happening to you" (4:12). God permits His children to be hammered on the anvil of suffering "so that the genuineness of your faith—being more precious than gold that, though perishable, is tested by fire—may be found to result in praise and glory and honor when Jesus Christ is revealed" (1:7).[50] We may pray to be spared the most intense forms of such testing, but either way, we can now endure in the certainty that all trials are permitted only for our good. Jesus has already gone into the furnace's fiery depths and, by His redemptive alchemy, transformed its hellish flames into burnishing purifiers. In the words of Karl Barth, "God has already done what we ask him."[51]

AND DELIVER US
FROM EVIL

"AND DELIVER US FROM EVIL"

I n the middle of the Rwandan civil war of the early 1990s, over the course of a mere one hundred days, almost a million members of the Tutsi community were murdered with machetes and rifles. It took the rest of the world time to come to grips with what had happened and eventually face its own complicity insofar as it had done nothing to stop the horror. When Canadian general Roméo Dallaire arrived as commander of the UN Assistance Mission to try to achieve a ceasefire, he witnessed firsthand the bloody hundred days: "In Rwanda I shook hands with the devil. I have seen him, I have smelled him and I have touched him."[52] Confronted with neighbors invading the homes of neighbors, raping and hacking them to pieces, we can't rely on abstract tropes about sin being present in every human heart. We need to speak about the demonic, about Satan. That is what Dallaire understood as he gaped at the piles of Tutsi corpses and witnessed the indifference of his fellow Westerners.

Jesus taught His followers to pray for deliverance from *the* evil—that is, the *one* who is evil, the ancient adversary of God, who, in the words of John Chrysostom, "wages against us an implacable war."[53] It's for this reason that some translations render this petition "Save us from the Evil One," with capital letters. "Evil has a definite physiognomy," as the liberation theologian Leonardo Boff puts it.[54] The Jesuit priest Alfred Delp, who was involved in a plot to assassinate Adolf Hitler, commented on the seventh petition from his Nazi prison cell: "There is not only evil in this world, there is also the evil one; not only a principle of negation but also a tough and formidable anti-Christ."[55] What we need to be rescued from isn't just the devices and desires of our own wayward hearts, as real and dangerous as those are, but also the malevolence of a personal being bent on our suffering.

In speaking this way, Jesus is in line with the entirety of the Bible. It may not in every place be as clear that the devil himself is in view, but the Bible everywhere speaks of evil not simply as pervasive but as *personal*. As early as the third chapter of Genesis, the origin of Adam and Eve's rebellion is depicted as a reasoning, speaking serpent (3:1). Job's torments are traced back to the instigation of a mysterious "accuser" (literally "the satan," in 1:6). The prophet Daniel is visited by an angel who reports a battle with "the prince of the kingdom of Persia" (10:13); Paul warns his converts that they must be prepared to contend "against the rulers, against the authorities, against the cosmic powers of this present darkness, against the spiritual forces of evil in the heavenly places" (Eph 6:12). Peter, likewise, tells his readers, "Like a roaring lion your adversary the devil prowls around, looking for someone to devour" (1 Pet 5:8). In the apocalyptic vision that closes the Bible's storyline, the defeat of ultimate evil is described like this: "And the devil who had deceived [the nations] was thrown into the lake of fire and sulfur" (Rev 20:10). And, above all, the New Testament portrays Jesus as having constantly to contend against a mighty and wily foe: "No one can enter a strong man's house and plunder his property without first tying up the strong man" (Mark 3:27). Scripture, in short, "has a penchant for personifying evil."[56] And when Jesus encourages His disciples to pray, "Deliver us from evil," it is most likely that it is this *personal* evil to which He refers.

But can modern Western people, who are skeptical of the efficacy of witchcraft and spiritualism, follow Jesus on this point? One of the fascinating developments in recent science, both in the hard sciences as well as the social sciences, has been the focus on how human beings are at all times at the mercy of powers greater than themselves. Contrary to sunny notions of free will and self-expression, we all are shaped by powers as small as microscopic biochemical forces, some of which are microbial interlopers in our bodies, to those as large as inherited notions of what constitutes acceptable gender performance.

Think, for instance, of how racism makes itself manifest in a society. Older generations of white Americans may have more readily thought, "So long as I am paying my black employee a fair wage and greeting her warmly each day, I'm not a racist." But racism operates more covertly and insidiously than that. In a recent experiment, for instance, a sociologist asked participants to stare at a screen on which a series of black and white faces flashed. These images appeared and disappeared so quickly that the viewers were not even consciously aware of having seen them. Immediately after seeing a black or white face, the participants were then shown a picture of a gun or a tool. These images were quickly removed from the screen but not quite as quickly as the facial images, so as to allow the participants to register having seen them. It turned out that when participants viewed a black face followed by a tool, they were more apt to remember the tool as having been a gun than they were when the image of a tool followed that of a white face. The racialized tendency to associate black faces with a violent weapon, the sociologist concluded, "requires no intentional racial animus, occurring even for those who are actively trying to avoid it."[57] People are, in a very real way, enslaved to something outside of their control. As one theorist has put it, racism has "a life of its own."[58]

So modern Western minds actually might be catching up with the inspired wisdom of Scripture rather than the other way around. Evil is not just what we *do*, but—more hauntingly—it is what we *suffer*, what we are mired in and encrusted with.

And if that is the case, we are unable to extricate ourselves from it by any direct action. No amount of good intentions—to return to our example from above—can cause a white person to disassociate black skin from the threat of harm. The prince of racism—and of so many other forms of evil—hinders even the most virtuous white people from ending their own racist habits of mind by sheer decision. Stronger medicine is needed. And that is what Jesus urges us to pray for: we must, in the end, appeal to God to deliver us from the grip of the Evil One. Christians who worship whiteness don't just need education; we need exorcism.

T he New Testament rustles with the news that God *already* has delivered us from the Evil One. Consider these words from the early Christian sermon that we know as the Letter to the Hebrews:

> The children of a family share the same flesh and blood; and so [Jesus] too shared ours, so that through death he might break the power of him who had death at his command, that is, the devil; and might liberate those who, through fear of death, had all their lifetime been in servitude. (2:14–15 NEB)

Making our mortal human nature His own, the Son of God died in order to defeat the Evil One who wielded death as a weapon. As the Orthodox liturgy says, He is "trampling down death by death."[59]

Or consider this from the First Letter of John: "The Son of God was revealed for this purpose, to destroy the works of the devil" (3:8). Or this, from the letter of Paul to the Colossians: Christ "disarmed the rulers and authorities and made a public example of them, triumphing over them in [the cross]" (2:15). Somehow, by dying, Jesus has rendered the devil impotent, denuding him of his ability to win the war he wages against human beings. There are different ways of thinking about how Jesus achieved this, and the New Testament uses a variety of different pictures or metaphors to help us see the full scope of His triumph over the Evil One. But the point all the images are seeking to drive home is that a decisive victory was secured in and through the events of Jesus' crucifixion and resurrection—a victory that sealed evil's fate once and for all, guaranteeing its final demise.

When we pray "Deliver us from evil," we are asking to be able to see, enjoy, and live in accord with what is true but still largely unseen in the present. We know that Jesus has already secured our final release from the Evil One, but we still sense evil's nearness and taste its effects. The victory of Jesus is real but not currently as visible as it one day will be. And so, in confidence but also in trembling and with tears, we pray for the final, public, irreversible experience of celebrating the defeat of the regime of our Enemy.

FOR THE KINGDOM,
THE POWER,
AND THE GLORY
ARE YOURS NOW AND FOREVER.
AMEN.

"FOR THE KINGDOM, THE POWER, AND THE GLORY ARE YOURS NOW AND FOREVER. AMEN."

One of the great slogans of the Protestant Reformation, made famous by Martin Luther's Wittenberg colleague and friend Philipp Melanchthon, goes like this: "To know Christ is to know his benefits."[60] Melanchthon's point was to stress that Christians shouldn't be too interested in bare facts about Jesus Christ. It isn't enough, for example, to know where He was born, or in what year, or how He preexisted the incarnation, or how His divine and human natures are in a mysterious personal union. As Melanchthon says, "Unless you know why Christ put on flesh and was nailed to the cross, what good will it do you to know merely the history about him?"[61]

Melanchthon was worried about a coldly scientific approach to knowing Christ that seemed to him to be represented by the theologians of his day. In place of that approach, he stressed that Christ is rightly known when we hear a preacher say aloud in church, "Almighty God in His mercy has given His Son to die for you and for His sake forgives you all your sins."[62] *That* is when we really *know* Christ—when we trust in Him for salvation and hear His words of assurance announced to us.

But in our day, we are especially vulnerable to a different error than the one Melanchthon tried to correct. For so long in Western theologies, we have focused most of our attention on all that we believe Christ provides for us—a clean conscience, say, or a restored marriage, a renewed work ethic, a reconciled community, the promise of justice and healing for the creation, and so on—that we have tended to forget the *aim* of all Christ's benefits: that we ultimately would be, as the hymn puts it, "lost in wonder, love, and praise."[63] Yes, pearly gates and golden streets will be lovely, but the point of all this heavenly imagery is to help us see that God Himself will be the Christian's eternal delight.[64]

When Pope Benedict XVI published the first volume of his trilogy of books on the life of Jesus, he introduced it with an arresting question: "What did Jesus actually bring, if not world peace, universal prosperity, and a better world? What has he brought?" What indeed? Surveying the sorry state of our world, we can sympathize with the Jewish philosopher Martin Buber's remark to one of his Christian friends on the eve of World War II: "We [Jews] know more deeply, more truly, that world history has not been turned upside down to its very foundations—that the world is not yet redeemed. We *sense* its unredeemedness."[65] So are we to conclude that Jesus effected no change in the world's situation, that His mission was a failure? Benedict XVI says no: "What has [Jesus] brought? The answer is very simple: God. He has brought God."[66] All of Jesus' life was oriented toward one goal: bringing human beings into a restored relationship with God so that they can behold God's glory forever, bathed in His radiant light and reflecting His worthiness back to Him in praise and adoration.

I t is God in Himself who pervades the final lines of the Lord's Prayer. If we have been praying in the previous few petitions for God to meet our needs for sustenance, forgiveness, and deliverance, our attention shifts in the final doxology as we simply attend to God's might and majesty. The incomparable King James Version renders it this way, capturing the way the Greek manuscripts foreground the divine pronoun: "For Thine is the kingdom, and the power, and the glory, for ever. Amen." Yes, God's kingly reign is for our benefit, and all His power is marshaled for the purpose of doing us good. But something more is in view here. The point isn't so much for us to ask God for more things but for us to realize that God transcends our limits and frustrations and that our saying so befits His splendor. Sarah Ruden puts it this way:

> We can expect to be saved from the devil because of this deity we invoked already, but now [at the end of the Lord's Prayer] there is more of the deity: he has not only a kingdom but power and glory. ... God is not just an entity coming into manifestation, invisible in the sky but with a name to be blessed, a kingdom to arrive, and a will to be enacted. His kingdom, power, and glory simply *are*, now and through eternity.[67]

This is what the final praise in the Lord's Prayer means to direct us toward: there is coming a time when we will have no more need to ask God for bread, for absolution, or for rescue. All of our tears will have been wiped away, death will have been finally defeated, and the earth and its people will be at peace and thriving. When that time comes, in the words of an old hymn,

> Hope shall change to glad fruition,
> Faith to sight, and prayer to praise.[68]

Petitions will not be necessary in God's future. We will cease asking God to supply our needs, since we will be entirely satisfied. All that will remain is to praise God—to enjoy His benevolent reign, to rejoice in what His power has achieved, and to see His glory. "Let it be so," which is what "Amen" amounts to, is the only appropriate response to these promises.

CODA

Praying the Lord's Prayer with Rembrandt

hen I moved into a house by myself after living in community for several years, one of the first things I did was order a framed print of Rembrandt van Rijn's *Return of the Prodigal Son*, the Dutch painter's memorialization of Jesus' parable of the runaway child and the forgiving father (Luke 15:11–32). I had read Henri Nouwen's pastoral meditation on Jesus' story and the painting, and it had moved me deeply.[69] I wanted to use the painting much as Nouwen had—as a daily reminder that I, a lost son, was beloved by a compassionate Father.

For a while the print hung over the fireplace in my living room. But then I moved again, and I decided to place it in a more private part of the house, on the wall space just above

the kneeler that I often use to pray. Now, whenever I bend my knees and rest my elbows on the wooden shelf, my eyes are almost level with the back of the son. I can look up slightly to focus on the Father's hands on the son's shoulders, and I can look into the Father's face.

Nouwen describes Rembrandt's memorable image so well:

> I saw a man in a great red cloak tenderly touching the shoulders of a disheveled boy kneeling before him. I could not take my eyes away. I felt drawn by the intimacy between the two figures, the warm red of the man's cloak, the golden yellow of the boy's tunic, and the mysterious light engulfing them both. But, most of all, it was the hands—the old man's hands—as they touched the boy's shoulders that reached me in a place where I had never been reached before.[70]

It's taken a couple of years for me to realize how much looking at this print hanging over my kneeler has affected the way I pray, too. In particular, I think, it's changed the way I pray the Lord's Prayer. Now, whenever I recite it, as often as not I'm looking at Rembrandt's image while I do. Each line has taken on new resonance.

Our Father, who art in heaven, hallowed be Thy name. To pray for the reverencing and uplifting of the Father's name is to pray that *this* welcoming, forgiving Father—the Father whose hands gently rest on His lost son's shoulders—be more widely known, seen for the compassionate Father that He is, and worshiped as the Giver of extravagant mercy. To pray for *this* Father's name to be hallowed is to pray that more lost sons and daughters find themselves kneeling under that gracious gaze.

Thy kingdom come, thy will be done on earth as it is in heaven. To pray for *this* Father's kingdom to come and *this* Father's will to be done is to pray for a reign of mercy, kindness, humility, and profligate divine generosity. It is to pray that debts would be remitted, rebellion ended with homecoming, and banquets held for the dissolute and the self-righteous alike. It is to pray not for the iron-fisted rule of a tyrant but for the self-giving reign of a Father who loves.

Give us this day our daily bread. To pray for regular sustenance from *this* Father is to pray to One who was ready to serve the best meat to a son who had already burned through half the family inheritance. To pray to *this* Father for daily bread is to receive not only the staples of life but also a filet mignon, not only water but also the best vintage. It is to receive abundance, lavishness, and generosity "immeasurably more than all we can ask or conceive" (Eph 3:20 NEB).

And forgive us our trespasses as we forgive those who trespass against us. To pray for forgiveness from *this* Father is to pray to One who leaps up and sprints toward us—throwing dignity to the wind—to offer us forgiveness before we have even been able to blubber our request for it. To pray for *this* Father's forgiveness is to barely get the words out before realizing we've been clothed with the finest garments the house has to offer.

To pray for our trespasses to be forgiven is to feel already this Father's warm tears as they drip down on our scabbed head.

And lead us not into temptation but deliver us from evil. To ask *this* Father to "deliver us from evil" is to pray to One whose hands and cloak provide shelter for us. Nouwen again: "With its warm color and its arch-like shape, [the Father's cloak] offers a welcome place where it is good to be. … But as I went on gazing at the red cloak, another image, stronger than that of a tent, came to me: the sheltering wings of the mother bird." To pray to *this* Father for protection is to pray to One whose character Jesus embodied when He wept, "Jerusalem, Jerusalem! … How often have I desired to gather your children together as a hen gathers her brood under her wings, and you were not willing!" (Matt 23:37).

For thine is the kingdom, and the power, and the glory, for ever and ever. Amen. To praise the kingship, the dominion, and the splendor of *this* Father is to praise the kingship of humility, the noncoercive dominion of nurturing love, and the radiant splendor of stooping and touching and embracing. To praise *this* Father "for ever and ever" is to acknowledge that such self-giving divine love is the fount of creation and redemption in eternity past and will be the theme of the lost son's songs into eternity future.

To pray the Our Father with Rembrandt and Jesus' Father in view is to find yourself praying it in a way you hope never to stop.[71]

ACKNOWLEDGMENTS

am grateful to all who read or heard portions of this book in manuscript form and gave feedback that helped me improve it: Mike Allen; Gary Beson; Deanna Briody; Matt Burdette; my parents, Walter and Suzanne Hill; Alan Jacobs; Jono Linebaugh; Orrey McFarland; Walter Moberly; Jamie Sosnowski; and Christopher Wells. I am also grateful to Todd Hains at Lexham Press, who first suggested I write on the Lord's Prayer and whose editorial input was received with gratitude.

I am especially appreciative to have been granted a sabbatical at the seminary where I teach, Trinity School for Ministry in Ambridge, Pennsylvania, which allowed me to complete the book.

Finally, my daily life, including my writing life, is sustained by the love of Aidan and Melanie Smith and their daughter—my goddaughter—Felicity. This book is dedicated to Felicity. We have already started praying the Lord's Prayer together, and I look forward, please God, to many more years of doing so. I love you so much, Fe.

ENDNOTES

1. Rowan Williams, *Meeting God in Paul* (London: SPCK, 2015). In the lecture given at Canterbury Cathedral in April of 2012 that was transcribed and edited for this volume, Williams used the word "cheek" after "nerve" which captures the idea memorably (Merriam-Webster gives "self-assurance" as one definition of "cheek").

2. Augustine, counting "Save us from the time of trial" and "Deliver us from evil" as two petitions, saw seven parts in the Lord's Prayer, while Origen, John Chrysostom, Gregory of Nyssa, and others collapsed those petitions into one, comprised of negative and positive counterparts. Although I think the latter position is more likely to be true to the Gospels' intent, I will follow Augustine in treating the negative and positive parts of the sixth petition separately.

3. Dale C. Allison, *The Sermon on the Mount: Inspiring the Moral Imagination* (New York: Crossroad, 1999), 22.

4. Allison, *The Sermon on the Mount*, 22.

5. Helmut Thielicke, *The Prayer that Spans the World: Sermons on the Lord's Prayer* (London: James Clarke, 1965), 22.

6. Sarah Ruden, *The Face of Water: A Translator on Beauty and Meaning in the Bible* (New York: Pantheon, 2017), 122–24.

7. Compare R. W. L. Moberly's remarks in his *Old Testament Theology: Reading the Hebrew Bible as Christian Scripture* (Grand Rapids: Baker Academic, 2013), 5.

8. In the Enuma Elish, the world is birthed from the intermingling of the fresh waters, portrayed as a god named Apsu, with the oceanic saline waters, the goddess Tiamat. See W. G. Lambert, *Babylonian Creation Myths* (Winona Lake, IN: Eisenbrauns, 2013), 3.

9. Robert G. Hamerton-Kelly, "God the Father in the Bible and in the Experience of Jesus: The State of the Question," in J. B. Metz, E. Schillebeeckx, and M. Lefabure, eds., *God as Father?* (New York: Seabury, 1981), 97.

10. Paul Ricoeur, "Fatherhood: From Phantasm to Symbol," in *The Conflict of Interpretations: Essays in Hermeneutics* (Evanston, IL: Northwestern University Press, 1974), 490–91. I am indebted to Janet Martin Soskice's reading of Ricoeur's essay in her essay "Calling God 'Father' " in *The Kindness of God: Metaphor, Gender, and Religious Language* (Oxford: Oxford University Press, 2007), 74–80.

11. See Deut 32:6; 2 Sam 7:14; 1 Chr 17:13; 22:10; 28:6; Pss 68:5; 89:26; Isa 63:16; 64:8; Jer 3:4, 19; 31:9; Mal 1:6; 2:10. On other occasions in the Old Testament, God is depicted in fatherly imagery but without the word "father" being used; see Exod 4:22–23; Deut 1:31; 8:5; 14:1; Ps 103:13; Jer 3:22; 31:20; Hosea 11:1–4; Mal 3:17. Other Jewish texts that were read and studied in the time of Jesus use "father" for God too: see, for instance, the *Qiddushin* tractate of the Babylonian Talmud, 36a; *Exodus Rabbah* 46.4.

12. The Council of Toledo (AD 675) puts it this way: "We must believe that the Son was not made out of nothing, nor out of some substance or other, but from the womb of the Father (*de utero Patris*), that is, that he was begotten or born (*genitus vel natus*) from the Father's own being." See Jacques Dupuis, ed., *The Christian Faith in the Doctrinal Documents of the Catholic Church* (New York: Alba House, 1982), 102–6.

13. "Our Father, you who are in heaven. ... With these words God wants to entice us, so that we come to believe he is truly our Father and we are truly his children, in order that we may ask him boldly and with complete confidence, just as loving children ask their loving father" (Martin Luther, *The Small Catechism*).

14. Karl Barth, *Prayer*, fiftieth anniversary edition (Louisville: Westminster John Knox, 2002), 22–23.

15. Stanley Hauerwas, *With the Grain of the Universe: The Church's Witness and Natural Theology* (Grand Rapids: Brazos, 2001), 28.

16. Janet Martin Soskice, *Kindness of God*, 76.

17. Dante Alighieri, *The Divine Comedy*, 11.1–2.

18. Sarah Coakley, *God, Sexuality, and the Self: An Essay "On the Trinity"* (Cambridge: Cambridge University Press, 2013), 327, 324.

19. Erich Auerbach, *Mimesis: The Representation of Reality in Western Literature*, trans. by Willard R. Trask (Princeton: Princeton University Press, 1953), 8.

20. Benedict XVI, *Jesus of Nazareth: From the Baptism in the Jordan to the Transfiguration* (New York: Doubleday, 2007), 143.

21. Nahum Sarna, *Exploring Exodus: The Origins of Biblical Israel* (New York: Schocken, 1986), 52.

22. Christopher R. Seitz, *Figured Out: Typology and Providence in Christian Scripture* (Louisville: Westminster John Knox, 2001), 143–44.

23. Simone Weil, *Waiting for God*, trans. Emma Craufurd (New York: Harper, 1973), 217.

24. *Martyrdom of Polycarp* 9.3.

25. Andrew Marin, *Love Is an Orientation: Elevating the Conversation with the Gay Community* (Downers Grove, IL: IVP, 2009), chapter 8. For more on the Marin Foundation's "I'm Sorry" campaign, see http://www.themarinfoundation.org/get-involved/im-sorry-campaign/.

26. C. Clifton Black, *The Lord's Prayer*, Interpretation (Louisville: Westminster John Knox, 2018), 97.

27. The classic statement is in Oscar Cullmann, *Christ and Time: The Primitive Christian Conception of Time and History* (Philadelphia: Westminster, 1964), 84.

28. Barth, *Prayer*, 39.

29. P. D. James, *The Private Patient: A Novel* (New York: Vintage, 2009), 349.

30. David Wells, "Prayer: Rebelling Against the Status Quo," *Christianity Today* (November 1979), 32–34.

31. This paragraph and parts of the following section are adapted from Wesley Hill, "Praying the Lord's Prayer in Gethsemane," *First Things*, April 2, 2015, https://www.firstthings.com/blogs/firstthoughts/2015/04/praying-the-lords-prayer-in-gethsemane.

32. William Nicholson, *Shadowlands: A Play* (New York: Penguin, 1990).

33. Timothy George, *Theology of the Reformers*, rev. ed. (Nashville: Broadman & Holman, 2013), 105.

34. F. D. Maurice, *The Lord's Prayer: Nine Sermons Preached in the Chapel of Lincoln's Inn*, fourth edition (London: Macmillan, 1861), 59, italics removed.

35. Maurice, *The Lord's Prayer*, 59, italics added.

36. Karl Barth, *Church Dogmatics* II.2, §38.2.

37. Weil, *Waiting for God*, 220.

38. I'm indebted to my colleague David Yeago for this insight.

39. "Article IX: Of Original or Birth Sin," in *The Book of Common Prayer* (New York: The Church Hymnal Corporation, 1979).

40. "A Penitential Order: Rite Two," in *The Book of Common Prayer*.

41. Augustine, *On Man's Perfection in Righteousness* 8.19: "For while there remains any remnant of the lust of the flesh, to be kept in check by the rein of continence, God is by no means loved with all one's soul."

42. "A Penitential Order: Rite Two."

43. Francis Spufford, *Unapologetic: Why, Despite Everything, Christianity Can Still Make Surprising Emotional Sense* (San Francisco: HarperOne, 2014), 48.

44. John Calvin, *Institutes of the Christian Religion* 3.20.45.

45. Calvin, *Institutes* 3.20.45.

46. Harriet Sherwood, "Lead Us Not into Mistranslation: Pope Wants Lord's Prayer Changed," *The Guardian*, December 8, 2017, https://www.theguardian.com/world/2017/dec/08/lead-us-not-into-mistranslation-pope-wants-lords-prayer-changed. Subsequently, the wording was officially changed; see Harriet Sherwood, "Led not into temptation: Pope approves change to Lord's Prayer," *The Guardian*, June 9, 2019, www.theguardian.com/world/2019/jun/06/led-not-into-temptation-pope-approves-change-to-lords-prayer.

47. See R. W. L. Moberly, *The Bible, Theology and Faith: A Study of Abraham and Jesus* (Cambridge: Cambridge University Press, 2000), chapter 3.

48. Hans Urs von Balthasar, *Mysterium Paschale*, trans. Aidan Nichols (San Francisco: Ignatius, 2000), 100.

49. The pope of the Coptic Orthodox Church subsequently announced the canonization of the twenty-one martyrs, and an icon written by Tony Rezk depicting crowns descending from heaven onto the martyrs' heads was widely shared on the internet.

50. My interpretation of the sixth petition is indebted to Daniel B. Wallace, "Pope Francis, the Lord's Prayer, and Bible Translation," https://danielbwallace.com/2017/12/12/pope-francis-the-lords-prayer-and-bible-translation/.

51. Barth, *Prayer*, 63.

52. Roméo Dallaire, *Shake Hands with the Devil: The Failure of Humanity in Rwanda* (New York: Carroll & Graf, 2004), xviii.

53. John Chrysostom, Homily 19.10 on Matthew.

54. Leonardo Boff, *The Lord's Prayer: The Prayer of Integral Liberation*, trans. Theodore Morrow (Maryknoll, NY: Orbis, 1983), 115.

55. Alfred Delp, *The Prison Meditations of Father Alfred Delp* (New York: Herder and Herder, 1963), 137.

56. Nicholas Ayo, *The Lord's Prayer* (Lanham, MD: Rowman & Littlefield, 2003 [1992]), 95.

57. B. Keith Payne, "Weapon Bias: Split-Second Decisions and Unintended Stereotyping," *Current Directions in Psychological Science* 15, no. 6 (2006): 287–91.

58. Eduardo Bonilla-Silva, *White Supremacy and Racism in the Post-Civil Rights Era* (Boulder, CO: Lynne Rienner, 2001), 45.

59. From the Paschal Troparion: "Christ is risen from the dead, / Trampling down death by death, / And upon those in the tombs / Bestowing life!"

60. Philipp Melanchthon, *Loci Communes* (1521), dedicatory epistle.

61. Melanchthon, *Loci Communes* (1521), dedicatory epistle.

62. I draw this language from the later *Lutheran Book of Worship* (Minneapolis: Augsburg Fortress, 1978).

63. Charles Wesley, "Love Divine, All Loves Excelling" (1747).

64. Some recent books have emphasized this point helpfully: Hans Boersma, *Seeing God: The Beatific Vision in Christian Tradition* (Grand Rapids: Eerdmans, 2018); Michael Allen, *Grounded in Heaven: Recentering Christian Life and Hope on God* (Grand Rapids: Eerdmans, 2018).

65. Quoted in Jürgen Moltmann, *The Way of Jesus Christ* (Minneapolis: Fortress, 1995), 28.

66. Benedict XVI, *Jesus of Nazareth*, 44.

67. Ruden, *The Face of Water*, 34.

68. Henry Francis Lyte, "Jesus, I My Cross Have Taken" (1824).

69. Henri Nouwen, *The Return of the Prodigal Son: A Story of Homecoming* (New York: Penguin, 1994).

70. Nouwen, *Return*, xx.

71. This coda is adapted from Wesley Hill, "Praying the 'Our Father' with Rembrandt," *Covenant* blog, September 23, 2015, https://livingchurch.org/covenant/2015/09/23/praying-our-father-rembrandt/.

TRANSLATIONS USED

Alighieri, Dante. *The Divine Comedy*. Translated by Allen Mandelbaum. New York: Knopf, 1995.

Augustine. *On Man's Perfection in Righteousness*. In *Nicene and Post-Nicene Fathers*, 28 vols. in two series, edited by Philip Schaff, 5:160–76. Buffalo, NY: Christian Literature, 1887–1894.

Calvin, John. *Institutes of the Christian Religion (1559)*. 2 vols. Edited by John T. McNeill. Translated by Ford Lewis Battles. Library of Christian Classics 20–21. Louisville: Westminster John Knox, 2006.

John Chrysostom. *The Homilies on the Gospel of St. Matthew*. In *Nicene and Post-Nicene Fathers*, 28 vols. in two series, edited by Philip Schaff, 10:1–510. Buffalo, NY: Christian Literature, 1887–1894.

Luther, Martin. *The Small Catechism*. In *The Book of Concord: The Confessions of the Evangelical Lutheran Church*, edited by Robert Kolb and Timothy J. Wengert, 347–63. Minneapolis: Fortress, 2000.

Melanchthon, Philipp. *Commonplaces: Loci Communes 1521*. Translated by Christian Preus. St. Louis: Concordia, 2014.

Martyrdom of Polycarp. In *The Apostolic Fathers,* vol. 1., translated and
edited by Bart D. Ehrman, 367–401. Loeb Classical Library 24.
Cambridge: Harvard University Press, 2003.

The Council of Toledo. "Symbol of Faith (675)." In *The Christian Faith in
the Doctrinal Documents of the Catholic Church,* edited by Jacques
Dupuis, 102–6. New York: Alba House, 1982.

WORKS CITED

Allen, Michael. *Grounded in Heaven: Recentering Christian Life and Hope on God*. Grand Rapids: Eerdmans, 2018.

Allison, Dale C. *The Sermon on the Mount: Inspiring the Moral Imagination*. New York: Crossroad, 1999.

Auerbach, Erich. *Mimesis: The Representation of Reality in Western Literature*. Translated by Willard R. Trask. Princeton: Princeton University Press, 1953.

Ayo, Nicholas. *The Lord's Prayer*. Lanham, MD: Rowman & Littlefield, 1992.

Balthasar, Hans Urs von. *Mysterium Paschale*. Translated by Aidan Nichols. San Francisco: Ignatius, 2000.

Barth, Karl. *Church Dogmatics*, vol. II, pt. 2. Translated by G. W. Bromiley. Edinburgh: T & T Clark, 2004.

———. *Prayer*. Translated by Sara F. Terrien. Fiftieth anniversary edition. Louisville: Westminster John Knox, 2002.

Benedict XVI. *Jesus of Nazareth: From the Baptism in the Jordan to the Transfiguration*. Translated by Adrian J. Walker. New York: Doubleday, 2007.

Black, C. Clifton. *The Lord's Prayer*. Interpretation. Louisville: Westminster John Knox, 2018.

Boersma, Hans. *Seeing God: The Beatific Vision in Christian Tradition*. Grand Rapids: Eerdmans, 2018.

Boff, Leonardo. *The Lord's Prayer: The Prayer of Integral Liberation*. Translated by Theodore Morrow. Maryknoll, NY: Orbis, 1983.

Bonilla-Silva, Eduardo. *White Supremacy and Racism in the Post-Civil Rights Era*. Boulder, CO: Lynne Rienner, 2001.

The Book of Common Prayer. New York: The Church Hymnal Corporation, 1979.

Coakley, Sarah. *God, Sexuality, and the Self: An Essay "On the Trinity."* Cambridge: Cambridge University Press, 2013.

Cullmann, Oscar. *Christ and Time: The Primitive Christian Conception of Time and History*. Translated by Floyd V. Filson. Philadelphia: Westminster, 1964.

Dallaire, Roméo. *Shake Hands with the Devil: The Failure of Humanity in Rwanda*. New York: Carroll & Graf, 2004.

Delp, Alfred. *The Prison Meditations of Father Alfred Delp*. New York: Herder and Herder, 1963.

George, Timothy. *Theology of the Reformers*. Revised ed. Nashville: B&H Academic, 2013.

Hamerton-Kelly, Robert G. "God the Father in the Bible and in the Experience of Jesus: The State of the Question." In *God as Father?*, edited by J. B. Metz, E. Schillebeeckx, and M. Lefabure, 95–162. New York: Seabury, 1981.

Hauerwas, Stanley. *With the Grain of the Universe: The Church's Witness and Natural Theology*. Grand Rapids: Brazos, 2001.

Hill, Wesley. "Praying the Lord's Prayer in Gethsemane." *First Things*, April 2, 2015. https://www.firstthings.com/blogs/firstthoughts/2015/04/praying-the-lords-prayer-in-gethsemane.

———. "Praying the 'Our Father' with Rembrandt." *Covenant* blog, September 23, 2015. https://livingchurch.org/covenant/2015/09/23/praying-our-father-rembrandt/.

James, P. D. *The Private Patient: A Novel*. New York: Vintage, 2009.

Lambert, W. G. *Babylonian Creation Myths*. Winona Lake, IN: Eisenbrauns, 2013.

Lutheran Book of Worship (Minneapolis: Augsburg Fortress, 1978).

Lyte, Henry Francis. "Jesus, I My Cross Have Taken" (1824).

Maurice, F. D. *The Lord's Prayer: Nine Sermons Preached in the Chapel of Lincoln's Inn*. 4th ed. London: Macmillan, 1861.

Moberly, R. W. L. *The Bible, Theology and Faith: A Study of Abraham and Jesus*. Cambridge: Cambridge University Press, 2000.

———. *Old Testament Theology: Reading the Hebrew Bible as Christian Scripture*. Grand Rapids: Baker Academic, 2013.

Moltmann, Jürgen. *The Way of Jesus Christ*. Minneapolis: Fortress, 1995.

Nicholson, William. *Shadowlands: A Play*. New York: Penguin, 1990.

Nouwen, Henri. *The Return of the Prodigal Son: A Story of Homecoming*. New York: Penguin, 1994.

Payne, B. Keith. "Weapon Bias: Split-Second Decisions and Unintended Stereotyping." *Current Directions in Psychological Science* 15, no. 6 (2006): 287–91.

Ricoeur, Paul. "Fatherhood: From Phantasm to Symbol." In *The Conflict of Interpretations: Essays in Hermeneutics*, edited by Don Ihde. Translated by Willis Domingo, Charles Freilich, Peter McCormick, Kathleen McLaughlin, Denis Savage, and Robert Sweeney. Evanston, IL: Northwestern University Press, 1974.

Ruden, Sarah. *The Face of Water: A Translator on Beauty and Meaning in the Bible*. New York: Pantheon, 2017.

Sarna, Nahum. *Exploring Exodus: The Origins of Biblical Israel*. New York: Schocken, 1986.

Seitz, Christopher R. *Figured Out: Typology and Providence in Christian Scripture*. Louisville: Westminster John Knox, 2001.

Sherwood, Harriet. "Lead Us Not into Mistranslation: Pope Wants Lord's Prayer Changed." *The Guardian*, December 8, 2017. https://www.theguardian.com/world/2017/dec/08/lead-us-not-into-mistranslation-pope-wants-lords-prayer-changed.

Soskice, Janet Martin. *The Kindness of God: Metaphor, Gender, and Religious Language.* Oxford: Oxford University Press, 2007.

Spufford, Francis. *Unapologetic: Why, Despite Everything, Christianity Can Still Make Surprising Emotional Sense.* San Francisco: HarperOne, 2014.

Thielicke, Helmut. *The Prayer that Spans the World: Sermons on the Lord's Prayer.* Translated by John W. Doberstein. London: James Clarke, 1965.

Wallace, Daniel B. "Pope Francis, the Lord's Prayer, and Bible Translation." December 12, 2017. https://danielbwallace.com/2017/12/12/pope-francis-the-lords-prayer-and-bible-translation/.

Weil, Simone. *Waiting for God.* Translated by Emma Craufurd. New York: Harper, 1973.

Wells, David. "Prayer: Rebelling Against the Status Quo." *Christianity Today* 23, no. 25 (November 2, 1979): 32–35.

Wesley, Charles. "Love Divine, All Loves Excelling" (1747).

Williams, Rowan. *Meeting God in Paul.* London: SPCK, 2015.

SCRIPTURE INDEX

Old Testament

NAME INDEX

The Christian Essentials series is set in TEN OLDSTYLE, designed by Robert Slimbach in 2017. This typeface is inspired by Italian humanist and Japanese calligraphy, blending energetic formality with fanciful elegance.

CHRISTIAN ESSENTIALS

The Christian Essentials series passes down tradition that matters. The ancient church was founded on basic biblical teachings and practices like the Ten Commandments, baptism, the Apostles' Creed, the Lord's Supper, the Lord's Prayer, and corporate worship. These basics of the Christian life have sustained and nurtured every generation of the faithful—from the apostles to today. The books in the Christian Essentials series open up the meaning of the foundations of our faith.

LEXHAM PRESS

For more information, visit
LexhamPress.com/Christian-Essentials